GET WITH THE PROGRAM

MARY NEWBY

New Degree Press

Copyright © 2020 Mary Newby
All rights reserved.

GET WITH THE PROGRAM

ISBN 978-1-64137-535-1 *Paperback*
      978-1-64137-536-8 *Kindle Ebook*
      978-1-64137-537-5 *Digital Ebook*

"Education is the passport to the future, for the future belongs to those who prepare for it today."

– MALCOLM X

CONTENTS

PREFACE.	TECH IS EVERYWHERE	7
INTRODUCTION.	HOW TO USE THIS BOOK	17
CHAPTER 1.	WHY COMPUTER SCIENCE?	19
CHAPTER 2.	TECHNOLOGY: THE PERFECT FIT FOR EVERY STUDENT	29
CHAPTER 3.	COMPUTER SCIENCE IN THE CLASSROOM	37
CHAPTER 4.	THE ROADBLOCKS	47
CHAPTER 5.	COMPUTER SCIENCE IN HIGH SCHOOL	55
CHAPTER 6.	TEACHING TEACHERS	65
CHAPTER 7.	COMPUTER SCIENCE IN ELEMENTARY SCHOOL	73
CHAPTER 8.	INTO THE CLASSROOM	79
CHAPTER 9.	LEARNING COMPUTER SCIENCE AS AN ADULT	87
CHAPTER 10.	TIME TO ACT	93
CONCLUSION.	WHAT NOW?	103
BIBLIOGRAPHY		105

PREFACE
TECH IS EVERYWHERE

Consider your daily routine. You wake up to your phone alarm and blink your eyes open. You check the weather to decide what to wear and respond to texts or emails you may have received while asleep. After getting ready for the day, you jump in the car, play your music, and get to work where you open your laptop and answer emails. Whether at work or at home, we all use our phones and computers throughout the day to check social media, place an Amazon order, text friends, and browse the internet.

All these things require code to work, and all this code was created by computer scientists. Our daily lives are surrounded by the work of computer scientists–from the phones we use, the cars we drive, our home security systems, our identity privacy, banks, grocery stores, the government, and so on. Human lives are so closely intertwined with technology that it's hard to imagine a world without it, and none of it would exist without the people who coded it.

Everyone knows that learning occurs both inside and outside of the classroom, but what about accessibility?

Unfortunately, computer science is *not* equitably accessible in both primary and secondary education as well as outside the classroom. Technology professional and creator of Habla Code Carlos Vasquez noticed the inequity of computer science in his community, and he has been working to change that ever since.

Carlos' younger sister attends high school in a primarily Hispanic neighborhood on the south side of Milwaukee, Wisconsin. Once a week her school has "Technology Hour," when each student learns basic computer science skills on the learning platform Code.org. She came home from school one day and appeared to be upset. When Carlos asked what was wrong, he learned that one of the students in her class could not participate in "Technology Hour" because Code.org was only offered in English, which the student did not speak. This language barrier simply removed the opportunity to learn about computer science from the student. This moment made Carlos aware of the inequity of computer science education and how Spanish speakers were particularly disadvantaged.

Several years ago, Carlos decided to enter the technology industry to help grow his career. As a native Spanish speaker, he noticed that almost all the computer science educational resources are only available in English. When he searched for Spanish coding tutorials and examples, he found limited responses, many of which were outdated. The lack of Spanish coding resources available also revealed the broader lack of Hispanic representation in technology industries. Carlos recalls, "I don't think I've gone to a [technology] networking event and talked to someone who is Hispanic."

This experience sparked Carlos' idea to create an application to teach coding in Spanish, which he calls "Habla Code." His goal with this app was not only to provide a Spanish resource to learn code, but also to create a safe and nurturing environment where learners aren't overwhelmed by the material or speed of the class.

In addition to creating this resource, Carlos also created his own text editor to make learning a coding language easier, more convenient, and more accessible. A text editor is a program in which coders can write, test, and deploy their code. Many times, text editors are separate applications that need to be downloaded onto a computer, and there are many options available. By having a text editor *within* the app, learners don't need to download any additional applications, making the process of learning code much more realistic for the learner.

In addition to teaching Spanish speakers coding languages like Java Script, CSS, and HTML, Carlos hopes that Habla Code encourages Spanish speakers to learn English. He wants this app to "spark an excitement to learn English, because much of code is done in English. And if they learn English, then they are able to help more people and create a bigger impact."

By breaking down the language barrier of learning computer science skills, Habla Code gets modern society that much closer to educational equity in technology. Carlos hopes that Habla Code "creates a community around technology for people who don't have access to a computer or can't have access because of a language barrier."

The reality is that while many people develop an interest in computer science at some point, they don't know how to pursue it. Unfortunately, that sets up a scenario in which it may be too late, and people lose interest. If Carlos hadn't intervened, his sister and her friends may never have studied computer science.

Carlos is focusing on Spanish-speaking communities, but what about other marginalized populations, such as African Americans, low-income or rural Americans, and women? How can we create 10,000 more Carloses who want the opportunity to learn computer science and are interested in extending its accessibility?

Computer scientists carry an immense amount of power. Through coding, they have the ability to shape the way people see the world, consume information, and communicate. Regardless of how you get your news–whether through an online news source, Facebook, or elsewhere–behind every platform is a computer scientist determining how you are going to get that information. It's a little scary that the world depends on computer scientists to accurately and fairly share information with them when, in reality, they are also just people. People make mistakes and have biases and personal interests, and all that influences the programming of technology we use on a daily basis.

That said, the world needs more (and better) computer scientists than ever before– computer scientists who will have the tough conversations about the impact of their work–from diverse backgrounds who can promote fairness and social justice in technology, and who understand their potential to change the world for the better. Thankfully, there are plenty of opportunities for more computer scientists.

The fields of technology and computer science are growing exponentially and are expected to keep growing. The U.S. Bureau of Labor and Statistics predicts that by 2026, over 550,000 new jobs will be added in the field.[1] These jobs are popping up in nearly every industry, including manufacturing, healthcare, business, retail, media, insurance, education, government, transportation, professional sports, and so on.

With so many industries utilizing machine learning and depending so heavily on software, it's no wonder technology and computing jobs are "the #1 source of new wages in the US."[2] There are currently more jobs available than there are trained technology workers to fill them.

According to these statistics from the US Bureau of Labor Statistics[3] and the National Center for Education Statistics (NCES)[4], the large number of computer science jobs available is wildly disproportionate to the percentage of graduates with the requisite skills to fill them.

---

1 "Computer and Information Technology Occupations: Occupational Outlook Handbook."
2 Ibid.
3 "Computer and Information Technology Occupations: Occupational Outlook Handbook." "Employment Projections."
4 "Computer and Information Technology Occupations: Occupational Outlook Handbook." "Data Trends."

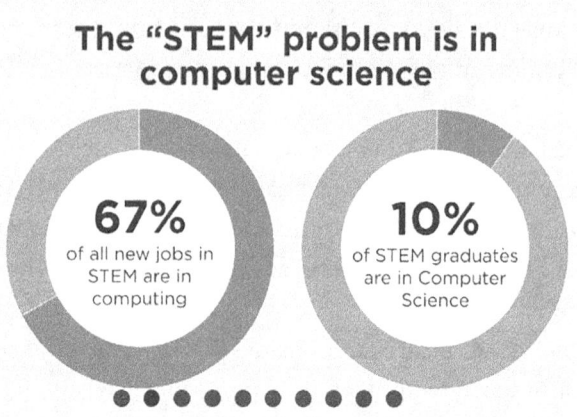

"What's Wrong with this Picture?"

These new tech jobs indicate how educational institutions need to not only equip students with the right training and opportunities, but also instill an interest in the field at a younger age. This is especially important in light of the rate at which technology is currently growing and moving. This speed of technology and innovation depends on the number of computer science professionals entering the workplace.

Companies and organizations are developing new and innovative solutions to everyday problems, but more computer science professionals are needed to execute these ideas. Without an influx of these professionals, innovation will progress more slowly, and ideas will be lost. That means ideas as small as eliminating glitches in your phone to ideas as big as solving climate change could be delayed by a sheer lack of employable computer scientists.

Many people are of the belief that computer science is only for the best and brightest students when, in fact, anyone with the right exposure, determination, and training can master it. Unfortunately, this belief means that students are often not exposed to computer science until college, because a large fraction high schools across the country don't offer the required courses. Exposing students to computer science skills at younger ages, even in elementary school, could spark more interest, passion, and excitement in the field.

I was called to write this book because there is an overwhelming misunderstanding of computer science education. Every student deserves the opportunity to learn computer science–regardless of whether the student loves coding or software development–because the skills are transferable and important. As a tech professional who took her first technology course in college, I found it difficult to ignore the lack of diversity. Making computer science education fully accessible instead of a privilege would open the floodgates to diversity in the field, which would in turn change the technology sector for the better.

At Marquette University in Milwaukee, Wisconsin, I pursued an independent study on technology integrated into early elementary education. That experience cultivated my passion for learning about technology in the classroom environment. After graduating with a degree in information technology, I worked as a technology professional in various positions at two Fortune 500 companies.

For the past two years, I volunteered for the Technology Education and Literacy in Schools K-12 program (TEALSk12), working as a teaching assistant for computer science courses in the Milwaukee Public Schools' district high schools.

Although I love education and computer science separately, my experience assisting in the classroom taught me that my knowledge and passion did not translate into being a good teacher.

After observing and admiring professional educators, I found it a shame that these teachers didn't understand computer science better because they were so much better than I at engaging and communicating with their students. That sparked my idea to raise awareness of the necessity of computer science education and educator training.

This book proposes various ideas about how to introduce computer science courses and skills into the classroom. Students of all ages can begin to learn about computer science, and with the growing integration of modern technology into our everyday lives, an understanding of computers has never been more relevant. I also discuss how computer science skills can be adapted by both children and adults outside the classroom. This book is primarily intended for educators and other education professionals, but it is also relevant to parents, technology professionals, those curious about the technology profession, and high school students. I want to emphasize the incredibly positive effects of integrating computer science into every classroom, along with equitable educational opportunities, increased diversity in one of the fastest growing fields, and so much more.

This book grapples with the difficulties of bringing computer science into the classroom, the hurdles teachers must jump through to become licensed as computer science teachers, and the embarrassing statistics about diversity in the field of technology. I will also discuss easy ways to integrate computer science into any classroom and what resources teachers can use to become better equipped to teach computer science.

INTRODUCTION

HOW TO USE THIS BOOK

This book is written for everyone, but feel free to tailor it to your needs. If you are reading something that doesn't speak to you, skip it! Some chapters directly address teachers, some address students, and others are aimed toward anyone with an interest in the direction of computer science education.

The structure of this book is as follows:

- Chapters 1–3 discuss the reasons behind the lack of computer science education.
- Chapters 4–6 examine the leg work required to integrate computer science in the classroom.
- Chapters 7–10 detail my recommendations for increasing computer science educational opportunities.

The best advice I can offer is to read what excites or challenges you. By educating ourselves on the topic, the general public can more effectively advocate for computer science education.

CHAPTER 1

WHY COMPUTER SCIENCE?

"Equality and equity are not synonymous."

–DR. LINDSEY OTT

At a *TED* Talk in 2017, Dr. Lindsey Ott discussed the difference between education equality and equity: "Equality is giving everybody a size 10 pair of shoes. Some people are going to be really excited about the size 10 pair of shoes, unless you don't wear a size 10. Equity is giving everyone a pair of shoes that fits."[5]

This distinction can easily be applied to education. All students must attend school to gain the knowledge, skills, and desire to pursue a future that will benefit themselves, their family, and the community. Whether preparing to go to college, learn a trade, or pursue a passion, an early education helps students to grow into successful adults.

---

5   Lindsey Ott, "Solving the Achievement gap."

However, the quality of that education–and the extent to which it fits the needs and desires of its students–has a tremendous impact. Students with different backgrounds, preferences, and skills need different approaches to education, and this is where equal education and equitable education diverge.

Whenever I tell people I'm in the tech sector, they usually respond along the lines of, "Wow, you must be really smart," or "Good for you, I'm terrible with computers!" Responses like these make me cringe a bit. This rhetoric completely isolates tech industries from anyone interested in it who doesn't think they are smart enough.

I'll be the first to tell you that I'm not a genius by any means. I worked hard in college for my 3.0 graduating GPA, which isn't bad but sure as hell isn't that of an "extremely gifted" student. Some might think, *"Why am I reading a book written by a mediocre student?"* However, I strongly believe that grades are not indicative of a person's success, and I'm not the only person with this perspective. In 2019, fifty colleges announced they will no longer require an ACT or SAT score for admissions because a standardized test score does not reveal a person's full potential or ability.[6] In spite of my less-than-stellar GPA, I have gained invaluable hands-on experience through my work, and my results now speak for themselves.

Here's the bottom line: the technology sector does not require inherent talent, perfect test scores, or a crazy amount of ambition. Though societal attitudes deem that only "geniuses"

---

6   Rebecca Safier,"Complete Guide: Colleges Not Requiring SAT Scores."

can pursue careers in tech, anyone with enough determination and interest can do it.

A BRIEF HISTORY

The history of computer science is essential to understanding the origins of this "genius" label on the tech sector.

Computer science, as we know it, has been around for more than seventy years, and it began with the digital computer machine created by IBM used during World War II to crack military codes. At the time, people were using physical switches to make this iteration work and, quite frankly, it did take a genius to create and maintain. As time went on and technology advanced, switches were replaced by universal programming languages and computer science was born.

In 1962, Purdue University introduced the first computer science program to its students. The 1970s saw the creation of pivotal languages including C and Pascal, and these influential languages paved the way for modern programming. In the 1980s, a tech company named Apple gave rise to the personal computer, which would ultimately become a modern staple inside homes across America. And that leads us to where we are today! (That's a short history and I'm skipping over a ton, but you get the gist.)

Since computer science is a comparatively new and rapidly-growing field, it stands to reason that there are still misconceptions about it. When the digital computer was created by IBM, it could only be used by extremely intelligent and highly-trained engineers. Even in the 70s, when popular programming languages were developed, students took several college courses in order to master them and bring them into applicable practice.

In today's world, computer technology has infiltrated nearly every field, computer science can be studied everywhere, and these skills have become ubiquitous. When your doctor sends a prescription to your pharmacist, you check the weather app on your phone, or you check out at a self-service grocery store counter, you are interacting with the work of a computer scientist. What this means is that the world needs more computer scientists–not only to maintain current technologies, but also the rate of advancement.

CHANGING THE CONVERSATION
In order to meet growing demand for these skills, we must change the common misconceptions about the field of computer science. As long as the field of computer science is heightened, people will be discouraged from pursuing it. So, how do we do this?

First and foremost, we must change the conversation, starting with students, because students are the future of the work force. Upon meeting someone in the computer science field, instead of marveling at their intelligence, people should ask more about what business they work for, what they do, and what projects they work on. Changing this conversation, especially in front of students, is the first step in promoting the accessibility of computer science as a career path.

We should also get excited about computer science jobs! Technology is growing at warp speeds, and a lot of it is really cool, but computer science is still stereotyped as work done crouched on your laptop in your mother's basement. It's important to have conversations about the broad span of opportunities or the incredible platforms that create our favorite products, websites, and apps. These conversations should primarily be held in the classroom.

Some schools are effectively enhancing and promoting technology skills, but other schools are still unable to provide any computer production courses and don't have the means of promoting careers in the tech sector. Unfortunately, schools with more funding usually have an easier time getting computer science courses into their curricula, whereas schools with less funding are more likely not to offer these courses. Unfortunately, this applies predominantly to schools in either urban, rural, low-income, or minority areas. If students in these communities do not have the opportunity to try computer science, pursuing a career in technology will require them to study it in college or learn these skills on their own. This can be done, but it is far more difficult.

With the recent boom in technology-related jobs, it is the responsibility of high schools to introduce computer science courses to their students before they graduate. A student's interest being sparked by a computer science course could be the start of a successful career path with plenty of job opportunities.

GRASSROOTS EFFORTS
In the absence of funding, it is solely up to teachers to advocate for the importance of computer science education and integrate it into their classrooms. This isn't extremely unusual, as the push for high school computer science education has been

largely a grassroots movement, led by teachers, parents, and citizens as opposed to the state governments or school administrations. Though this is an amazing movement, the need for additional support of computer science in schools persists, as governments are unlikely to mandate these programs.

This begs the question: could businesses bring computer science education to diverse communities? The technology sector as a whole suffers from a lack of diversity, likely because the requisite courses are often not available to students in diverse high schools. It is in the best interest of technology companies to notice the lack of diversity and become stronger advocates for change. By sponsoring computer science teacher trainings and workshops, technology companies could make a considerable impact in bringing more students to the field. It is the responsibility of both schools and tech companies to bring computer science into diverse classrooms and alleviate the disparity of diversity in the field.

EDUCATIONAL EQUITY
In the discussion of educational equity in tech and computer science education, I must first loudly echo what education scholars and advocates have said before: educational equity is *not* the same as educational equality.

In the context of education, equality does not account for the individual needs and circumstances of each student. A person's experience, perspective, opportunities, and challenges all influence their interpretation of equality and must be accounted for in order to achieve equity.

Take a look at the following image:

"Illustrating Equality Versus Equity."

Each person in this picture has the common goal of watching the baseball game over the wooden fence. However, each person has different needs that must be met in order to see the game. The person on the left can see the game just fine because he is naturally tall enough to see over the fence. The person in the middle needs just a little help to see over the fence. On the other hand, the person to the right needs much more help in order to see over the fence. In an equality-driven educational model, individual needs are not taken into account, whereas an equity-driven model accounts for individual needs and adjusts accordingly.

THE ACHIEVEMENT GAP

Some students come into the classroom inclined to pay attention, complete their homework on time, and obtain decent exam marks. Other students struggle with holding attention, have problematic home lives making homework difficult or less of a priority, or go to bed hungry, all of which might contribute to poor exam performance. Although every school has students with different levels of ability, the achievement gap enables us to understand how these levels are influenced by other factors.

The Glossary of Education Reform defines the achievement gap as, "any significant and persistent disparity in academic performance or educational attainment between different groups of students, such as white students and minorities, for example, or students from higher-income and lower-income households." [7] Conversations are held at the national level about closing the achievement gap, but a one-size-fits-all solution does not exist. For example, the economic achievement gap will have a different solution than the race achievement gap, which might require different changes than the gender achievement gap. By understanding the achievement gap, teachers, school administration, and policy makers can make informed and advantageous decisions to make education more equitable for all students.

What does equitable education and the achievement gap have to do with technology? As I mentioned, the technology sector lacks diversity. In fact, in the United States in 2016, 75.3% of students graduating with an Information Technology (IT)-related degree were male.[8] Additionally, 44.6% of the students graduating in 2016 were white.[9] According to

---

7   Brandi Johnson, "Achievement gap."
8   "Information Technology." Data USA.
9   Ibid.

recent numbers from the College Board National and State Summary Reports, only twenty-two percent of students in AP Computer Science are women, and only thirteen percent are African American or Hispanic/Latino.[10] The following charts provide more information:

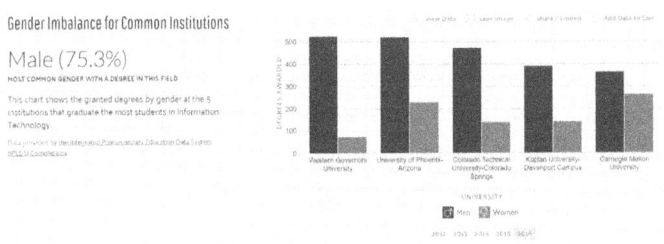

"Information Technology." Data USA.

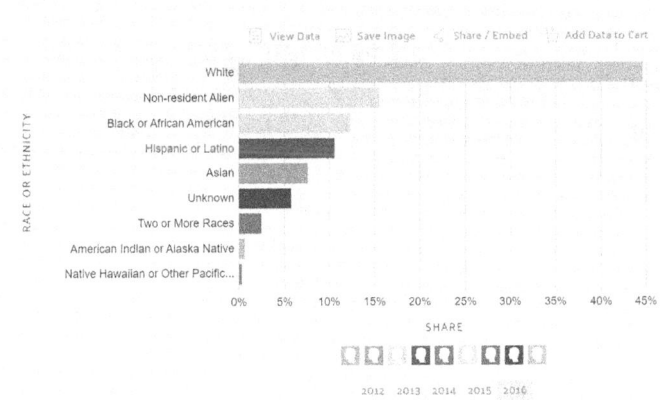

"Information Technology." Data USA.

---

10   "AP Data Overview." Research College Board.

The students negatively affected by the achievement gap are the same students underrepresented in the technology sector. In order to both close the achievement gap and diversify the technology sector, education must be made more accessible, tailored, and desirable for all students, regardless of race, gender, or economic status. Computer science is broadly applicable to other industries like healthcare, hospitality, the media, and professional sports. If schools and teachers can determine how to best tailor technology courses for their students and capture their attention, I believe that the technology field can become much more diverse in a short amount of time.

Broadening the availability of computer science courses and learning opportunities would bring the United States closer to closing the achievement gap and diversifying the tech sector. Though actually implementing these plans presents some difficulties, it is not impossible. It's going to take some work, but it'll be worth it!

CHAPTER 2
TECHNOLOGY: THE PERFECT FIT FOR EVERY STUDENT

Technology is an amazing field to be in right now because it is exponentially growing, constantly innovating, and always exciting. Though I've truly felt lucky to be a part of it, I still felt an itch to give back and give my work more purpose. This is what led me to an opportunity with Technology Education and Literacy in Schools (TEALS).

TEALS is a volunteer organization that connects technology professionals looking to teach computer science to willing schools. Volunteers like me visit high school classrooms once or twice a week for first hour of the day to train teachers with little to no computer science teaching experience. After class, I go to work and begin my day just like any other. The thought is that my field experience and technical knowledge of the subject helps teachers in introducing the material to their students. After two years of guided teaching with a technology professional, each teacher should be well equipped to teach the computer science course on their own. My time volunteering with TEALS for the past two years has positively changed the way I look at computer science education and my job performance.

During these two years, I have been at two different schools in the Milwaukee Public Schools (MPS) system and served a diverse, primarily low-income set of students. Admittedly, these students had a much different upbringing than my own. I come from a white, upper middle-class family, attended a private college preparatory high school, and was expected to earn a degree from a reputable college for which my parents would help me pay. Although my own high school was minutes away from these high schools, the students' lives were foreign to me.

I grew up thinking that the only way to be successful was to attend college and receive a bachelor's degree, but my students have taught me much more about the necessity of college.

NOT EVERYONE IS BORN A STUDENT
It is foolish to expect everyone to succeed in a classroom setting. As mentioned previously, I was not the strongest student. My parents enrolled me in a college-preparatory high school and helped me improve my writing, studying, and test taking, and I would still call myself a decent student at best. In spite of this, I fought my way through school to get into college and eventually graduate school. But different people possess different talents, some of which may not align with the skills needed to succeed in school.

The classroom environment can also be difficult. Students are expected to sit silently and listen to an adult lecture on topics they may or may not be interested in for six hours a day. That doesn't work for many students, and if students do not see their potential in that environment, why would they continue? College isn't for everyone because not everyone is born a student.

COLLEGE IS EXPENSIVE

This isn't a groundbreaking fact, let alone unique to the United States. As of 2018, students in the United States owed over $1.5 trillion in student loan debt, and that number is growing.[11] Among my graduating class in 2017, the average student left with about $28,000 in student loans.[12] This is oddly close to the exact amount I owed upon graduation, even with my parents' help!

My students often ask me how I paid for an education at a private college like Marquette University. I was honestly only able to afford it because I earned a great scholarship and my parents helped me significantly. Saying this to my students breaks my heart because scholarships rarely cover the costs that accompany a college education–like books and room and board–and there is only a slim chance that their parents have the means to help.

Beginning adulthood life with tens or hundreds of thousands of dollars in student loans hanging over your head is less than ideal. The burden of being in a huge amount of debt for years and years discourages some people from pursuing a college degree at all.

---

11 "Student Loan Debt Statistics 2019."
12 Ibid.

YOU DON'T NEED A COLLEGE DEGREE TO HAVE A GREAT CAREER

One of the high schools where I volunteer is a technical high school. Technical high schools value and teach technical skills to the same degree as academic skills, enabling students to choose the best career path upon graduation. All the knowledge needed to succeed as a mechanic or electrician, for example, is taught right in school. To some high schoolers, securing a well-paying job right after school instead of plunging into debt sounds like a pretty good deal.

According to Indeed.com, "The average Skilled Trades salary ranges from approximately $45,760 per year for Crew Foreman to $122,573 per year for General Manager."[13] The students I teach in Wisconsin may know that the Governor who served from 2011-2019 doesn't have a college degree, either. These facts and figures about trade jobs and jobs that don't require a degree may be enticing to some graduating students, because we all know money talks. College isn't for everyone, and a college degree isn't necessarily required in order to have a great career. I think I've made my point.

Regarding the technology sector, you do not need a degree in Computer Science in order to become a successful software developer or technology professional. My manager has been in the technology field for twenty years, first as a programmer and then as a manager in data management. After receiving his degree in biology and discovering he didn't want a job in that field, he took a handful of computer programming courses until he felt competent enough with the information.

---

13 "Trade and Skilled Trades."

He has since built a successful career in technology at a Fortune 500 company.

Computer science is a great degree option for those with the opportunity and the means. However, high schools that promote skilled trade jobs after graduation don't always include software development as a viable option. According to Glassdoor, the average salary for a software engineer is a little over $100,000 a year.[14] Not only is the pay great, but the job opportunities at companies big and small are endless and all over the world.

High schools with predominantly workforce-bound students have the unique opportunity to position their students for success in a skilled career in software development, as this is a skill anyone can learn as long as the opportunity is available.

The lack of available computer science teachers begs the question of why tech professionals don't just teach with TEALS as I do. This is due to the fact that technology professionals are not trained teachers. When I joined the TEALS program, I naively thought that perhaps technical professionals or technical retirees could teach computer science and make up for the lack of teachers qualified to teach the subject. After about one month in the classroom actually teaching high school students, I quickly learned why that was a bad idea.

A *DEVELOPER*, NOT A TEACHER
I could go on about why a technology professional like me should not be dropped into a classroom to do a teacher's job.

---
14 "Software Engineer Salaries."

It took a lot of energy and plenty of embarrassment to learn these lessons, so I'd like to share my takeaways with you.

First of all, teachers are trained in how to engage students and keep their attention for longer than thirty seconds. While some computer science professionals may have tutored or taught computer science at a local community college, teaching high school is a different game. In high school, it's unlikely that every student wants to be in the class at all. Some students are placed in a class by their counselor and have to grin and bear it for the semester. As someone who has a lot of excitement for technology, this was a bummer.

On top of that, some students walking into the classroom seemed to be sick of a class that hadn't even started yet, which posed a big challenge. It was a shot to the heart when I realized that I had to teach students who truly hate computer science, and I still have no idea how to pull that one off. Maybe a magic trick? Bribery? I'm really willing to try anything. The worst part is, I don't know how to make myself sound interesting! (Please don't stop reading this book–I promise I'll keep things interesting for you.) Sometimes a personal anecdote will grab their attention, but it's a little trickier when discussing something like programming loops.

Another skill of many teachers that I certainly don't possess is an understanding of student individuation. In a classroom full of students, each is on a slightly different page. During a given lesson, some students may already know the material and are bored, while other students don't yet understand what happened yesterday! Differentiating lessons and activities for students on all levels is something I struggle with but am working on.

A MASTER AT ANSWERING QUESTIONS
One of the most impressive skills I've seen in teachers is the art of answering questions. When a student asks me a question, I give them a direct answer and the problem is solved. The student is happy, and I feel smart. However, as I have learned from my fellow teachers, that is not an effective way to teach. Framing answers to questions to guide the student toward the answer is a difficult thing to remember when you're also giving point blank answers in the workplace five days a week. When a colleague asks me a question in the office, there's not a chance I am looking to teach them anything! That's not my job. When I'm in the classroom, however, that is exactly my job. I plan to change this habit through further practice and teacher observation.

The last thing I learned is that students aren't always that nice. In the workplace everyone is cordial even if they absolutely hate you, because that's the way offices work. In school, on the other hand, some students don't feel the need to be nice and will tell it straight to your face. (Don't worry, I'm totally cool about it. I don't even care that a student pointed out that I looked especially tired today and that I should try concealer. Totally cool about it. This is something teachers face all the time and I applaud them for this because it really takes a toll on a person's self-esteem. And by the way, I do know what concealer is–I'm just too lazy to use it every day.)

My point is that there is a reason for requiring teachers to obtain a college degree and/or licensure. Teaching is a discipline that takes practice and patience. It is silly to think that any professional can walk into a classroom and teach a class with the same professionalism, engagement, and ease as a seasoned teacher. I am still in awe of how talented the teachers I work with in TEALS are, and I feel lucky to learn from them.

A VIABLE SOLUTION
The solution to a lack of computer science teachers is not to replace teachers with technology professionals and call it a day. That would be disastrous. Instead, teachers should be trained to teach computer science so they can utilize their teaching prowess to transfer the same information.

CHAPTER 3
COMPUTER SCIENCE IN THE CLASSROOM

In my conversations with people about technology pedagogy, I realized there's a huge gap in understanding between consuming technology and producing technology.

While researching for this book, I asked education professionals–including teachers, administrators, and principals–about how their students learn about technology. I began to see a recurring theme in their responses: "we have Chromebooks in the classroom" or "the students take turns using iPads" or "the students are growing up around technology."

Kids are starting to become comfortable and confident using technology at progressively younger ages. I recently witnessed my sister and niece get into the classic parent-child fight about the right age to get a cell phone. (I recall having the same fight with my parents when I was in high school.) It went something like this:

Me: So, what do you want for your birthday?

My niece: Well, I really want a phone, but my *Mom* won't let me have one.

My sister: Nope, I don't think you're old enough for a phone yet.

My niece: But *all* my friends have them!

My sister: Yeah, and I think that's weird!

Here's the catch: my sister was having this argument with her daughter who is nine years old and in the fourth grade. (I sincerely hope your eyes just bugged out of your head a little.) That is the reality we're living in–technology is everywhere, and it's being used at home, in the workplace, and even in the classroom by people of every age.

CONSUMING VERSUS PRODUCING TECHNOLOGY

Students being able to use (or "consume") technology is not what I'm most concerned about. What I *am* concerned about is students' ability to create (or "produce") their own technology and learn these skills through coursework or experience. Though most schools do offer technology classes, they unfortunately tend to focus on technology consumption. Granted, consumption is an important aspect of technology, but so much lies beyond that! If all of technology is a puzzle that creates one big beautiful picture, then consumption is just one small piece. The other pieces include:

- networks
- databases
- software development

- hardware
- infrastructure

In many of the schools I've worked with, their technology programs consisted solely of a typing course. Don't get me wrong–typing is a broadly applicable and beneficial skill–but offering it as the sole technology course presents a misunderstanding of technology and its potential.

(To be honest, I gained most of my typing skills through AOL Instant Messenger or AIM, which was all the rage in middle school. And let me tell you, nothing gets you typing faster than chatting with your crush before your mom calls you for dinner.)

Typing is about repetition and practice, whereas technology concerns patterns and logic. Both are important, but they teach different skills.

It's time to focus on the *production* of technology as well as the consumption of it. Though technology consumption is easy to understand, technology production is far more advanced. Most teachers would be capable of teaching a typing lesson, for example, but far fewer would feel comfortable teaching a computer science lesson.

While helping teach Introduction to Computer Science at a local high school, the teacher asked an interesting question: "How is computer science a science class?" This was a great question, because I'd honestly never given it any thought. In fact, I'd never even grouped science classes like biology, chemistry, or physics together with computer science. In my mind, they were separate entities, despite being grouped together under "science." That said, the student responses blew me away, not only in their complexity, but also their thoughtfulness and creativity.

"How is computer science a science class?"

First student: Solving problems through knowledge and formulas.

Second student: Making educated guesses about how to solve a problem and revising that guess if you get it wrong.

Third student: Using the scientific method to create and test a theory.

All the answers pointed to specific problem-solving methods. This reinforced my belief that students must be given the opportunity to learn computer science in order to cultivate creative and unique ways of thinking. Computer science is extraordinary because it allows students to think differently, solve problems creatively, and identify patterns to speed up work in ways unlike what they've seen in any class before.

A computer science class fosters rare and incomparable learning skills that are highly relevant to today's job market. When schools invest in a robust technology program including technology production and consumption courses, students are able to take full advantage of these exciting and valuable lessons.

I feel inclined to point out that schools are not to blame for the misunderstanding between technology consumption and technology production. Faculty and staff are led to believe that by equipping their students with laptops and tablets and teaching them how to use them successfully, they've fulfilled students' technology education needs. People tend to notice the presence of technology in grocery stores and hospitals, but not how that technology is created in the first place. Through investing in computer science courses, schools can change the conversation about technology and positively impact both their students and community.

With all the other material and skills students learn within the span of a school day, it is hard to imagine having much room for another course, especially one as intense as computer science. This begs the question . . .

WHERE DOES COMPUTER SCIENCE FIT IN?

Let's think about the concept of school itself. A person begins school at a young age to learn how to socialize, compromise, understand, and adapt. As the student gets older, they acquire knowledge that challenges them, stimulates critical thinking, and promotes problem solving. In learning this knowledge, students get a feeling for what they like, where they excel, and what career path they'd like to pursue. The classes taken by high school students usually fall into one of the following categories:

- English
- Reading
- Math
- Science

English provides the foundation for understanding the complexity and power of language, and students are greatly benefited by these classes. English classes teach students to communicate effectively in utilizing proper sentence structure, understanding grammar, and composing original work. These skills are necessary in every student's personal and professional life, enabling them to share their talents and gifts with the world.

If the subject of English is how ideas are communicated, then reading classes are how those ideas are consumed. Reading opens students' minds, fosters critical thinking, and is essential to a student's education.

Math courses teach students to solve problems in an environment in which there is often a finite answer. An analytical mind is needed to examine a problem, determine the best way to find the answer, and correctly execute that technique. Additionally (pun intended), math is used everywhere, including non-academic scenarios like filing taxes, refinancing loans, balancing a checkbook, or even betting on a horse at the Kentucky Derby. Math skills enable students to solve different kinds of problems in multiple ways, which makes it a critical subject for study.

According to the Oxford Dictionary, science is "the intellectual and practical activity encompassing the systematic study of the structure and behavior of the physical and natural world through observation and experiment." Science examines the world around us and explains the workings of the universe. Whether students are learning chemistry, astronomy, or physics, science classes teach students to explore the "why" and "how" of the world and thus gain a new perspective. By practicing the scientific method, students can ask a multitude of questions and systematically find answers.

WHAT DO THESE SUBJECTS HAVE IN COMMON?
These subjects comprise a student's educational foundation. However, they do not provide every academic skill that a student might need. During my second year of college, I took a philosophy class, and it was the first time I'd ever formally studied logic. This way of thinking, which focused on cause and effect, drew and held my attention. Upon entering the technology sector, I began to see it everywhere. This seemed like a skill that I should have learned prior to college; however, logic (taught in computer science classes) was not available in my high school. I aim to change that.

In college, it took me two years to declare a major because I couldn't figure out what I wanted to do with the rest of my life. I was always told to do something I was passionate about, but I didn't know exactly what that was. In many cases, students establish and grow passions in school based on their interests, talents, and experiences within the classroom. For me, this happened when I was a sophomore in college during my first technology class. In my case, simply having the opportunity was essential to choosing my path.

When I was in school, there were no required computer science courses or elective courses for that matter. But in today's technology-driven world, technology courses should be more robust, inclusive, and widely available to students.

UNDERSTANDING THE DILEMMA

Technology is everywhere, and it is not going away. Children are being exposed to technology earlier than previously thought imaginable. It is intertwined so deeply with everyday life that it has become second nature to both adults and children. From our cell phones and TVs to our doorbells and grocery store checkouts, nearly everything is a computer in one way or another. So, if our kids can't avoid technology, why aren't we teaching them how it all works?

Computer science education activist and professor Dennis Brylow shares this same concern for his children during our interview. He says, "Technology is everywhere, and we are constantly consuming it. If I could give my kids the tools to produce this technology, they could create any future they wanted, regardless of the field." He is right! Technology is fundamentally changing the way all work is done. If we can teach students the skills needed to manufacture and develop tech, they can bring those skills and knowledge to any field of interest.

What amazes me most is that computer science education courses are unlike any other course currently taught. Computer science is often compared to math or science when it is actually not much like either. Though computer science is probably more math- and science-oriented than it is related to English and reading, it differs too much to be grouped into either subject. Math *is* involved because computer science involves utilizing formulas to calculate solutions, and science *is* involved when students experiment, test, and validate hypotheses. But these examples are a mere fraction of what comprises computer science education.

SOFTWARE DEVELOPMENT

As a school subject, software development offers a unique set of lessons and skills, and it's exciting. Students use apps on their phones all the time, which piques their curiosity as to whether they could create one themselves. Software development requires a deep understanding of a particular language, its logic, and the cause and effect of programming on development.[15] While development requires analytical problem solving, it also requires patience, resilience, and creativity to find out-of-the-box solutions to difficult problems.

Understanding logic is key to learning a software development language. Logic is an extremely unique subject that, as I mentioned, I only began to study in college. Like I said before, software development is just a piece of this computer science education puzzle, but if this much can be learned in one class, imagine the potential. If students start learning these tactical and soft skills at an early age, they will be better positioned for success in their future.

Computer science education is so exciting because it has enormous potential to positively affect students' lives. I want

---

15   Much like spoken languages, coding is communicated in various written languages. Coding languages come in many different varieties (like Java, C#, or Python), and each is used to communicate with computer software in different ways. Languages are what enable you to click on your inbox and check your email, process your payment on Amazon, and many, many other things. Each language communicates using unique commands and formulas. Some languages are similar, and others are not, but they are always evolving to encompass more capabilities.

to start putting more computer science classes into the classroom right now! If only it were that easy.

There are numerous roadblocks hindering schools from investing in computer science classes. These changes require time, motivation, and resources, and although a long road lies ahead, we must start somewhere.

CHAPTER 4

THE ROADBLOCKS

When I decided to write a book about increasing technology courses in classrooms across the nation, an idea struck me. I thought I had found the answer to finding tens of thousands of new teachers capable of teaching computer science, and I couldn't believe I was the first to think of it.

Here is my big idea: colleges and universities should offer computer science teaching as a subject in their teaching certification programs or schools of education! Genius.

I started the interview process for this book by speaking to Bill Henk, the Dean of the College of Education at Marquette University, my alma mater. My plan was to pitch this idea, and for Dean Henk to be struck by my incredible genius. After speaking with Bill and doing quite a bit of research, I realized the impracticality of this idea.

In my defense, my thought process was that if more teachers were certified to teach computer science right out of college, it may be easier for schools to provide computer science courses. One major issue in computer science education is an extreme lack of teachers, so giving teachers the certification right out of school seems like a simple solution! (Oh Mary, you should have known there was so much more to it than that.)

Bill Henk has been in the education profession for over thirty years, with over fifteen of those years as Dean of the College of Education at Marquette University. We only had an hour to talk, so the plan was to explain the book I wanted to write and pitch my stroke of genius. However, the entire conversation barely went past my explanation, as Bill interjected with many comments and concerns.

Here's the thing: I know technology. I've studied it, taught it, worked in it, and truly tried to immerse myself in it. That said, I have a lot to learn about the world of education. It's fortuitous that I was able to speak to Bill first, because he raised three potential roadblocks to introducing computer science into education curricula.

ROADBLOCK #1: REQUIRED CREDITS

My idea of adding a few courses to the college curriculum seemed so simple and efficient in my mind–a quick fix. But like most tough situations, reality is far more complicated.

According to Bill, "Institutions are in a crunch to put enough materials within the four years students are in school. There is a push to bring all higher ed systems to 120 credits." This means that colleges will need to strategically *minimize* the number of classes needed to graduate while still fulfilling state licensing regulations for teachers.

This kind of put the kibosh on my idea of adding more classes to the education department curriculum. But there is hope! Bill says offering an elective on computer science education is always an option, and though it's not ideal, at least it's a start.

ROADBLOCK #2: CREDIBILITY
<u>Designing credible courses is more difficult than it sounds.</u> Bill told me, "Institutions need to comply with state agencies that regulate accreditation of courses. If a course hasn't been accredited, (the institution) won't teach it because it's not in its best interest."

I will return to the difficulty that comes with trying to create credible courses to qualify teachers to teach computer science courses, but this was my first wake-up call to the hoops I'd have to jump through.

ROADBLOCK #3: TEACHER INTEREST
To be frank, I hadn't considered the interests of teachers in my plan. Teachers balance multiple responsibilities, and not every teacher will be as enthusiastic about computer science as I am. (I know, shocking!) Thus, I conducted a kind of process of elimination to determine which teachers are likely to have an interest in learning and teaching computer science skills.

1. I'd argue to eliminate all elementary education teachers from the equation. You do not need any license or course completion to teach some capacity of computer science to children in elementary school, so it's safe to say teachers will not want to waste their time or money in a computer science education course. However, this is not to say that

elementary teachers shouldn't bring computer science into the classroom just not a license! But I'll get to that later.
2. Of the secondary education teachers, let's eliminate every teacher that is not specialized in a subject related to science, technology, engineering, or mathematics (STEM). This is not to say that English or writing teachers wouldn't be interested in teaching computer science, but for the sake of numbers, I'm going to assume that most will not.
3. Let's optimistically estimate that fifty percent of STEM teachers possess some interest in teaching computer science. It's safe to say we're dealing with a small subset of teachers. But Bill assures me that these teachers are worth pursuing: "Technology is a part of everyday life as a part of the culture. What concerns education students is the question of 'is this something that can give me a job . . . or even a higher paying job?'" A background in teaching computer science courses will likely give educators a leg up due to demand.

A lot of work still needs to be done in advocating for computer science education. As I came back to reality and saw the issue in all its complexity, I abandoned my bright idea as a one-size-fits-all solution.

LACK OF MOTIVATION

In my interviews, I also spoke with countless teachers and school administration about computer science education training opportunities. Many raised the issue of teacher motivation. In contemporary society, we ask a lot of teachers. They ensure our students are safe, included, happy, comfortable, and accepted while simultaneously designing and teaching engaging and challenging lessons. And all of that is just while the student is inside the classroom!

Teachers are also expected to provide a clean, inviting, and motivating workspace for, prepare activities and games to keep class interesting, grade the work of students fairly and accurately, answer parent and administrative emails in a timely manner, and be available before and after school in case something comes up. Oh, and for all the tiring and thankless work teachers do, they are inadequately paid and recognized. I am exhausted just writing all this.

While I just provided a laundry list of reasons why being a teacher is exhausting, it is also one of the most rewarding and crucial careers. Every society desperately needs gifted teachers to instill wisdom, kindness, and knowledge into their students. I honestly think being a teacher is one of the more selfless, generous, and impactful careers.

The point of my ranting on about all the responsibilities of teachers is to make it extremely clear that teachers are juggling a lot of balls. And yet here I am, telling teachers to spend even more of their time learning something that won't even be relevant in five to ten years because of how fast technology changes! The audacity.

I admit that I understand why teachers would not want to invest in learning how to teach computer science. Teachers have already proven to me that they are superheroes disguised as educators. When it comes to teaching computer science, what's in it for them?

Computer science is broadly applicable and beneficial to whatever career a student pursues. Skills taught in computer science cannot be found in any other subject, and this knowledge would help students to become better thinkers and problem solvers in the future. Overall, that's really the entire point of teaching. Let me paint you a picture.

Bella is a second-year high school student in urban Chicago. She comes from a low-income neighborhood, is the oldest of four, and works part time after school. She does well enough in school, but schoolwork isn't her highest priority amid all of her responsibilities. Bella's counselor notices that she struggles with traditional math classes and enrolls her in Introduction to Computer Science as an alternative course to fulfill her math requirement.

Bella is nervous and, quite frankly, uninterested in computer science. She never liked computer games that much, doesn't really know what computer science is, and heard it was a tough class. It's safe to say her motivation plummets before ever stepping foot into the classroom.

Bella goes to class every day and is surprised to find that her teacher talks about computer science in a way that makes sense. Bella uses her classmates when she needs guidance, and her teacher shows her how to easily look up examples of code. Plus, the projects and games she creates are actually pretty cool.

The teacher notices her interest in computer science and recommends she join a local coding club like Girls Who Code, where she can meet other girls her age who share a similar interest. After attending club meetings, becoming friends with other coders, and going to hack-a-thon events held by local companies, Bella envisions her future as a software developer. She later applies to several college computer science programs and gets in with a scholarship for being a woman in tech. Four years later she becomes the first person in her family to graduate college, is a role model for her younger siblings, escapes the poverty cycle, and becomes a successful computer programmer.

Though that story is not real, it could be. Students with early exposure to computer science are more likely to take a course or continue their education in technology. Teachers ultimately give students a great advantage by investing in computer science opportunities for their classrooms, and access to those opportunities could change a student's life.

Lastly, it's worth mentioning that the ability to teach computer science is a competitive bargaining tool. Schools need computer science courses, and teachers with the skills to teach it are attractive candidates for higher salaries or to teach in a wider range of schools.

From a young age, students want to grow up and have a cool job–maybe as a firefighter or race car driver, or maybe a doctor! But the job opportunities available in computer science are plentiful and–I must admit–really cool. Tech careers are also extremely relevant. It's not rocket science to know that students want to learn about topics that are relevant in their lives and to society. Computer science topics will capture the interest of students because they intersect with their daily lives. Though integrating computer science might be asking a lot of schools, teachers, and existing curriculum, it just might be worth it.

CHAPTER 5
COMPUTER SCIENCE IN HIGH SCHOOL

"Education is the passport to the future, for tomorrow belongs to those who prepare for it today."

—MALCOLM X

A JUGGLING ACT

Introducing a new school subject is a juggling act. Take a pretty good juggler, the kind of juggler who performed at your local Memorial Day parade, but never went traveling with the circus or anything that serious. We're going to name the juggler Computer Science Education (clever name, I know, but I want to make my point super clear, so go with it).

Computer Science Education is always juggling three balls: the school administration, teachers, and students. CS Education has gotten really good at juggling these three and can do it with little trouble. But a fourth ball–parent concern–also comes into play, and a fifth ball–government accreditation–is also in the air.

Computer Science Education struggles to keep all five balls in the air at once. Other factors to consider include:

- competitive job opportunities for teachers
- advance class licensing
- funding!

Successfully integrating computer science programs into high schools entails addressing a lot of moving parts. In addition to educating and motivating teachers to bring more computer science skills into the classroom, it takes alignment from school administration, parents, and more to make it a reality.

TALKING TO COMPUTER EXPERTS
To better understand the hardships of bringing computer science courses and qualified teachers into the high school classroom, I spoke to Dr. Dennis Brylow, a longtime computer science education advocate and computer science professor. Dennis teaches computer science at Marquette University and works to educate and train teachers in computer science. His interest began in high school, which continued into an undergraduate major, followed by a master's degree and, eventually, a computer science PhD.

While pursuing his PhD at Purdue University, Dennis' peers recognized and discussed the importance of seeking out STEM teachers who showed interest in computer science and giving them the tools and support to teach computer science courses. After earning his PhD and starting at Marquette University in 2005, Dennis continued that pursuit and started collecting data on the number of computer science teachers in the state of Wisconsin.

Because Wisconsin did not have state data on the number of advanced level high school computer science teachers, Dennis had to seek it out himself. He concluded that there were about 32 Advance Placement (AP) level computer science teachers in Wisconsin out of the 700 high schools in the state. That means under five percent of all high schools in the state of Wisconsin had a qualified advanced level computer science teacher.

This number is disappointingly low for computer science education advocates like Dennis and me because we believe *every* high school should offer computer science opportunities to *all* students. My high school did not offer a computer science course while I was in attendance, but now students can take many computer science classes, and I am extremely proud. Luckily, I had the time and resources to take a technology elective in college, but not everyone has that option. Dennis took this issue into his own hands and dug deeper into how and why this issue persists.

The first problem Dennis noticed was schools' understanding of what technology in a school means. There is a big difference between being a consumer of technology and being a producer of technology, and schools didn't differentiate between the two. Many schools would think they were excelling in technology because every student had access to a Chromebook, even when failing to provide a single computer science course to students.

Dennis also noticed the utter lack of computer science teachers available. This was magnified when considering the aforementioned number of advanced computer science teachers in Wisconsin. To combat this, Dennis has sought out teachers in other subject areas, both STEM and otherwise, to teach them the skills and provide resources for teaching computer science in their schools.

Dennis wanted to establish standards for computer science teachers in the state, but he knew that would mean he'd have to work within Wisconsin's education regulations to successfully implement them. So, he partnered with the Computer Science Teachers Association (CSTA) to establish the Wisconsin chapter of the organization. The CSTA is a group of computer science teachers who share resources, provide advice, and advocate for more computer science teachers and courses. By establishing a CSTA branch in Wisconsin, Dennis gained access to a support system that would aid in his goal of increasing access to computer science education in high schools.

Through the help of this organization, Dennis applied for a federal grant with a goal of doubling the number of computer science teachers in Wisconsin in a four-year window. Although Dennis did not receive the $1M-dollar grant the first and second time he applied, the third time was the charm.

And thank goodness he didn't give up applying. With the grant money, Dennis began the Computer Science for High School (CS4HS) program. CS4HS is a two-week workshop that trains educators in how to teach multiple levels of computer science courses. Although a $1M grant seems like a large amount of money to work with, Dennis still receives help from Code.org and other organizations to sponsor the class with scholarship and class materials. CS4HS also offers workshops for high school teachers to learn how to implement computer science education.

With the help of Code.org, teachers of kindergarten through eighth grade can attend the "Exploring Computer Science" workshop for free, which covers how to integrate technology skills like pattern recognition and coding basics. In addition to Code.org sponsorship, teachers attending other CS4HS workshops that are not free to attend can also receive scholarship dollars from Microsoft Tech Spark, Google, and other technology groups to fund these workshops.

Dennis is clearly working extremely hard to create optimal opportunities for teachers to learn how to introduce computer science courses to their schools, but it takes more than just learning the skill to implement it in the classroom. About fifteen years ago, the state of Wisconsin changed their teacher accreditation system and required every high school teacher to demonstrate proficiency in teaching student-specific skills.

For example, math teachers now need to demonstrate how to teach calculus skills as well as their own proficiency in calculus. To enforce this new educator requirement, standards were created for various subjects like math, physics, English, and biology.

At the time this law was put into place, there were no standards for computer science, meaning that it was literally impossible for computer science teachers to demonstrate their proficiency. With this law, the top ten education colleges in the state ended their programs for computer science educators. (Major bummer.)

To combat this, Dennis sat as a co-chair on the computer science standards committee; this committee established standards so that computer science teachers could continue to teach with an official proficiency in teaching computer science. After standards were established, Wisconsin became the ninth state in the nation to approve K-12 academic standards for computer science educators. (A round of applause for Wisconsin!) Currently, thirty four out of fifty states now have computer science education standards.

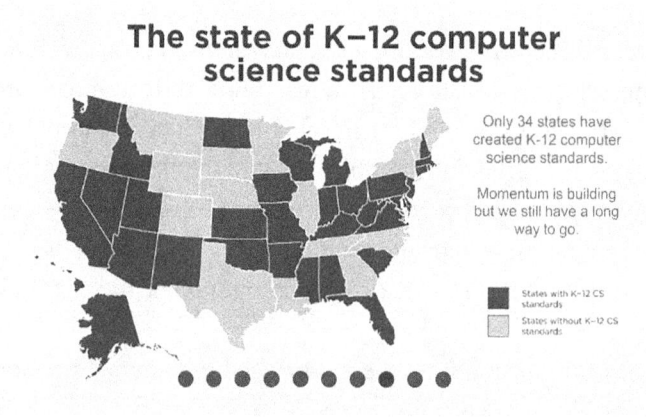

"Blurbs and Useful Stats."

The proficiency standards were not the only legal hurdle Dennis had to jump. Wisconsin requires an academic license to teach computer science at the advanced level–such as the Advanced Placement (AP) courses that are eligible for college credits. Dennis likes that educators must have a license to teach advanced level computer science courses because having a well-qualified teacher benefits students.

But, in his words, "It's a double-edged sword." If the state makes it difficult for other STEM teachers to get their license, it runs the risk of decreasing the number of AP computer science classes available for students.

CS4HS WORKSHOPS FOR TEACHERS

Dr. Dennis Brylow wants to create an easier pathway for teachers who want to earn their advanced-level computer science license. The CS4HS program also offers a course that prepares teachers to take and pass the accreditation exam. This exam can be taken by any educator wishing to be licensed as an advanced computer science teacher, but it is not easy. Dennis said, "This exam would take about three to four computer science courses at a college level to confidently pass it the first time." As a technology professional, I honestly don't know if I would be able to pass it my first time around.

Another way to earn the license is through a methods course on how to teach computer science effectively in the classroom. The CS4HS workshop offers this course that spans over one year; several universities in Wisconsin also offer the course as an elective in their curriculum.

The CS4HS workshops run during the summer in Milwaukee, the biggest city in Wisconsin. For those of you who don't know, Milwaukee is in the southeast part of the state, about an hour and a half north of Chicago. Its location makes access extremely difficult for the rural parts of the state–particularly the northern region–because getting there entails a four- to six-hour drive.

As I mentioned in the previous chapter, the education system asks a lot of teachers, and this process–taking time and money to drive to Milwaukee, stay in a hotel, and cover all accompanying costs in their time off–is a tall order. Dennis spoke to me about his concerns about bringing computer science to rural areas and how he's working to resolve this issue.

Dennis travels with his CS4HS daily workshops to reach rural cities throughout the state and the Upper Peninsula (UP) of Michigan. According to Dennis, many of these schools also don't want to implement computer science courses because they say students need to improve and speed up their typing skills first. Dennis rebukes this train of thought: "What are the presumptions about what your students are going to do if typing is more important than computer science? No computer scientist lost their job because they typed too slow."

While this is a compelling argument for computer science advocates, I also understand why schools find typing classes important. I believe the argument that typing classes and computer science classes fall under the same category is a misunderstanding. Both are important in pursuing successful careers, but they are not related beyond the fact that each utilizes a keyboard. Instead, schools should give students every opportunity to be successful by teaching both skills. Giving students options to grow and pursue passions is what makes schools successful.

The push for computer science courses in Wisconsin is currently a grassroots movement led by motivated teachers. Dennis says that "school administrators are usually the last on board when it comes to bringing in new computer science courses." To be fair, school administrations also juggle a lot of responsibilities. Since computer science education is not a primary concern among school administrators, it usually slips through the cracks.

The curriculum of Wisconsin schools is locally controlled by each area's school district. Unfortunately, no school district is required to offer computer science course or to even incorporate computer science skills. Therefore, advocating for these courses and skills is an individual battle with each of the 400+ school districts–each with their own goals and incentives.

Licensing, on the other hand, is controlled by the state, and there is a legislative push to loosen licensing requirements to increase the number of teachers. However, Dennis fears that "those teachers may not be as effective as when the licensing was tougher to get."

Beyond attaining a computer science teaching license, it is even more difficult to be an active computer science teacher. Because computer science is new to most schools, and schools typically only have one computer science teacher in the first place, it is unlikely that schools will have a computer science department.

Without a department, a teacher does not have a community or resources among other teachers in the school, making their job even tougher. The CSTA hopes to create that virtual community among computer science teachers, but it is still a difficult hurdle. Technology is also constantly changing, so teachers who commit to teaching computer science must understand that the current material may be completely obsolete in five to ten years.

My conversation with Dennis helped me to better understand the constant battle between state and local government over computer science in the classroom. He has worked for years and dedicated the better part of his career to training more computer science teachers and promoting early exposure among younger students. This chapter provides only a glimpse into the work that is currently being done and remains to be done in order to integrate computer science in the classroom, and this is only one state.

This begs the question: Where do we go from here? Do we put pressure on education colleges to include computer science licensing? Or do we mandate on a state and local level that all schools must have at least one computer science course available to high school students? What if that doesn't work?

The one thing that is clear is that teachers must do the work to learn computer science, become proficient enough to teach it, and convince their schools that computer science courses are worth it. Thank goodness for academics like Dennis who've dedicated themselves to the effort.

CHAPTER 6
TEACHING TEACHERS

Clearly, schools, teachers, and students face many obstacles in offering, teaching, and learning computer science. One of the biggest hurdles seems to be keeping the teachers in the classroom. According to the Learning Policy Institute, about eight percent of teachers leave the profession every year.[16] Teaching is a difficult profession, and new opportunities enticing teachers with higher pay and fewer hours may pull them away from education. Teachers with computer science training may be particularly persuaded by opportunities with other tech employers. Convincing a teacher to take on computer science education is a challenge, but the hardships don't stop there.

A common fear about bringing computer science into schools is that oftentimes, only one teacher in an entire school is teaching the subject. This means that if the teacher leaves, a school loses the computer science component of the curriculum entirely. Former TEALS Milwaukee Regional Manager

---

16 D. Carver-Thomas and L. Darling-Hammond, *Teacher Turnover: Why it Matters and What We Can Do About It.*

Mark Zachar also worries about teacher attrition. "It's common for teachers to come and go and in computer science. That means that when the teacher goes the class dies with them," Mark says.

Mark knows this story all too well. He used to be a high school computer science teacher until he took a job at TEALS. TEALS[17] philosophy is that every student deserves the opportunity to study computer science in high school. Unfortunately, Mark had to sacrifice the computer science program he started at his school in order to accept the TEALS job. That said, the impact of Mark's work with TEALS and the increase in pay to support his family of four were important factors.

The issue of opportunity cost came up several times in my interviews with various computer science advocates. Dr. Dennis Brylow (introduced in Chapter 5) experienced issues like Mark's.

Dennis had the unique opportunity to take a computer science course in high school during the early 1990s, and those classes established an interest that flourished into a passionate career. Dennis spoke fondly of his high school computer science teacher, calling him "ahead of his time and doing a great service for his high school." Unfortunately, when Dennis' high school teacher tragically passed away, the computer science program ceased to exist. This meant that the computer science program that inspired Dennis' lifelong career would no longer be able to influence future students.

---

17 "About TEALS - What Is TEALS?" "What We Stand For."

CAREER & OPPORTUNITY CHANGES

As is true of other fields, it is not uncommon for teachers to leave schools. The global analytics and consulting firm Gallup has called millennials the "job-hopping generation," meaning that this trend isn't likely to end any time soon.[18] Additionally, if a teacher learns the skills to teach computer science, that qualifies them for better paying jobs at higher paying schools or businesses.

Teachers, because of their selfless nature, often want to do the work for the betterment of their students and will put in the work in order to bring these opportunities to their students and community. That said, a school program should not depend solely on one teacher's hard work to establish, grow, and maintain it.

There are small ways schools can support their teachers that make a huge impact. Departments, for example. Just like there are departments for math, science, and English, when a school takes on computer science classes, there should be a department for teachers, or the single teacher, to rely on.

Understandably, not every school has the resources to support a new department, and it is a great accomplishment to even have one teacher dedicated to teaching some, or all, computer science classes. However, there are resources and commitments schools can support before taking on computer science classes. And the best part is, they're super easy!

---

18   Amy Adkins, "Millennials: The Job-Hopping Generation."

WHAT RESOURCES SHOULD BE AVAILABLE TO TEACHERS?

First, teachers should have access to resources and support from other teachers. Educational communities also make teaching a new subject more inviting and less overwhelming. The Computer Science Teachers Association (CSTA) provides support and tools to teachers as well as creates a camaraderie within the community. Also, it's an inexpensive resource, costing only $50 annually for a single teacher. Encouraging and sponsoring teachers to join the CSTA and to look to them for resources will promote confidence in themselves and the work they are doing. It should be said that a school providing this help and small monetary contribution demonstrates to the teacher that the school cares. Not to mention, computer science is a constantly innovating field with new and exciting changes every day. Having a support system to keep both students and teachers excited about the material will keep the teacher engaged and the students interested and continuing to enroll.

Second, schools should consider hiring more computer science teachers and establishing a program so that (a) more computer science courses are available to students, (b) teachers can rely on each other to create content and a program tailored to schools' and students' needs and goals, and (c) if one teacher is to leave, the computer science program is not in jeopardy. It is extremely difficult to find one teacher who wants to be the sole provider of computer science education at a school. But, when a plan is in place to grow more teachers, it gives both the teachers and the program confidence. A computer science program will also benefit the school with having more diverse class options and a variety of ways to engage student interest.

Last, although it is the most expensive tool, providing teachers financial incentives to teach computer science could be considered. If schools were to offer incentives for investing in learning computer science education, more teachers may be more willing to try. Taking on being the sole computer science teacher at the school takes a lot of time, effort, and energy. Oftentimes, it is perceived as a big challenge with little support. With incentives to become a computer science teacher, the teachers feel that their hard work is being both recognized and appreciated. This is important in order to keep teachers at their school instead of taking other jobs.

Keeping teachers satisfied at work and with their career should be a priority for school administrations struggling to retain teachers. The chart below demonstrates that job dissatisfaction is by far the number one reason teachers leave the profession.

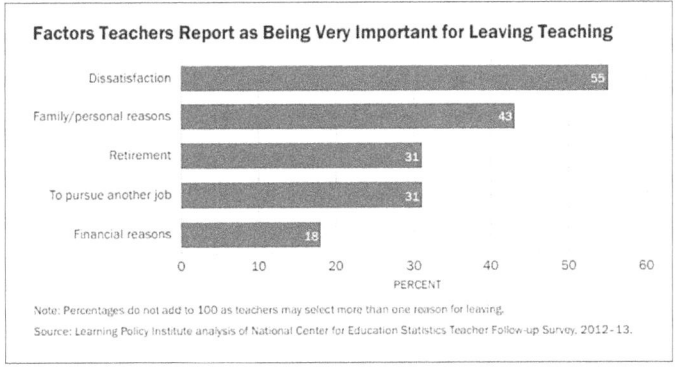

"Information Technology."

INCENTIVES FOR TEACHERS

Computer science education is in high demand, and if teachers take the time to learn this skill, they should be recognized for their work. Incentives could include paid time off (PTO), pay increase, benefits, and more. Teachers and school administration would need to discuss and negotiate appropriate compensation.

Obviously, the first step is to hire more computer science teachers. Once more teachers enter the schools, attention and care must be paid to keep them happy and encourage them to stay. Teaching is often a thankless job and asking them to take on any more responsibilities is typically a big ask.

But if financial incentives are impossible, simple things like recognition and appreciation can go a long way. If schools are able to thank their teachers for their efforts (which in turn benefits the students), these teachers will be more likely to continue improvements and stay at their school. Showing appreciation also doesn't have to be an expensive gesture. A simple, personal thank you card, recognizing teacher's accomplishments at a meeting, or thanking them in person with a smile can go a long way. I'm not saying these simple gestures will always keep your teachers from pursuing other work, but gratitude never hurts.

Throughout this section I have been speaking to schools and school administration for the most part. But I feel that it is important for everyone to know more about what teachers do and the sacrifices they make to teach our students.

It's also important that people see the high expectations of schools to keep teachers, students, and parents happy. This can be extremely difficult especially when funding is low, and options are few.

On top of balancing all their duties, teachers are pushed to constantly improve with little reward or recognition. One might ask, are there easy ways to implement computer science education without consuming all our schools' resources? The short answer is yes. The longer but still short answer is yes, but like anything, it will take encouragement and support.

Later, I'll discuss rational, realistic ways to implement positive changes and create more computer science learning opportunities. But for now, let's brighten things up a bit!

CHAPTER 7

COMPUTER SCIENCE IN ELEMENTARY SCHOOL

"You will either step forward into growth, or you will step backwards into safety."

—ABRAHAM MASLOW

Now for the moment we've all been waiting for: How the hell are we actually going to implement computer science into the classroom?

Ideally, every school would offer courses in computer science and technology for every grade. Realistically, that's not possible, at least any time soon. In the meantime, I want to discuss how every level of education could integrate computer science courses, skills, or awareness into the classroom and existing courses.

Let's start at the beginning of the education journey: elementary school. Just like core subjects such as English, math, reading, and science, computer science education can be taught at the elementary level. Granted, I am not expecting elementary aged students to be learning software development languages. (Side note: that would be awesome. If anyone knows of a second-grade programming application let me know, because that's sweet!) But fundamental skills and broad awareness can be taught at a younger age which lead to teenage students' interest in technology-related fields.

Something important to note when integrating technology into elementary education is that at this age, children are learning how to produce and consume technology at the same time. Students nowadays are surrounded by technology in every facet of their lives, and it is the responsibility of both parents and schools to teach young people how to safely and responsibly consume it. If we leave this crucial part of technology education out of schools, students and their peers are left to their own devices.

As a millennial who grew up alongside rapidly-developing technology, I know firsthand that elementary students who don't know how to safely navigate computers, phones, or the internet end up doing foolish things later–posting a picture of their house or home address, sharing when they will be home alone, encountering inappropriate sites online, or worse.

When used responsibly and for good, technology is an awesome tool. So, let's teach students about safe technology use and introduce them to computer science while we're at it.

LET'S GET INVOLVED

My friend and old co-worker Joe Ribbich works as a tech project manager for a Fortune 500 company. We recently went for coffee and discussed early exposure to technology. Joe has three school-aged sons and is an involved parent. He speaks to his experience with his sons' Cub Scout troops and praises the Boy Scouts of America organization for keeping up with the times. To my happy surprise, the Boy Scouts have merit badges as well as entire camps dedicated to STEM.

The Boy Scouts aren't alone in their efforts to introduce technology skills to elementary-aged students. Joe is also involved with his FIRST Robotics program, in which he and his sons are challenged to complete different projects and objects on computers and tablets usually with Legos. The encouragement of STEM by big brands like LEGO is essential for grabbing the interest and attention of young students.

IN THE CLASSROOM
Youth brands like LEGO and the Boy Scouts of America see the need for technology education at an early age, but that realization has yet to reach our education system. Funding is one reason for this. School districts tight on resources cannot or will not shell out money for computers or tablets so that every student can practice computer science skills in class. That is not a rational solution. However, schools and teachers are getting creative in teaching technology consumption and computer science to their students.

Many classrooms use a handful of desktop computers and tablets that are shared and passed around by multiple students. Classrooms with these technologies could take advantage of the many free computer science education resources on the internet.

Code.org specializes in providing free resources to students, teachers, and anyone wanting to learn computer science. As previously mentioned, Code.org is also a big contributor to Dr. Dennis Brylow's CS4HS workshops. Their online platform offers many engaging computer science lessons and activities for elementary-aged children.

Beyond Code.org, parents and educators may choose from *many* other applications on tablets and smartphones that teach children to code through games and activities. These games are simple, fun, and engaging for younger students, and they teach students how to both consume and produce technology. Although allowing a first grader a computer may not be realistic for all school districts, there are other ways to engage students in technology activities, and most of them not even involving technology! Teachers can find countless resources such as those below to foster computer science skills without any technology in front of them.

CSunplugged.org is a free resource for teachers with lessons, games, activities, and conversations that promote a different way of thinking and tying it in to computer science. These technology free activities are vital for elementary-aged students to engage and truly understand the underlying concepts of computer science, so I encourage them at schools with or without hardware availability.

Many other organizations run workshops during the summer and throughout the year for teachers to study computer science implementation. As mentioned in Chapter 5, Dr. Dennis Brylow runs the CS4HS workshops throughout his summer in the Milwaukee area. He works tirelessly with school districts and sponsors to ensure teachers' pay little to nothing and leave the workshop ready to teach these concepts in their classrooms. People like Dennis are all over the nation, so be sure to research your own local advocates.

Any teacher–regardless of computer science or technology background–has the ability to teach computer science. It is my hope that all elementary teachers also take a sincere interest in teaching these skills because they are so vital to students. With technology appearing everywhere we turn and technology careers expanding exponentially, it is vital that we supply our students with the means to succeed.

Although playing these games and asking these questions at a young age may seem insignificant compared to the rest of a student's educational career, fostering an interest in these skills early on is important.

OUTSIDE THE CLASSROOM
If you are a parent or guardian of an elementary school-aged student (or just a nosy aunt like me), many computer science activities successfully engage students outside of the classroom.

As an aunt of six amazing nieces and nephews, and often a designated babysitter, I have frequently sought anything to distract the kids from running around the house or destroying whatever is in my purse. In this day and age, the easiest way to distract a child is to throw a smartphone or a tablet in front of them. What's awesome about technology right now is that there are thousands of apps, any of which are both fun and sneakily educational. Like drinking a fruit smoothie that somehow has a handful of spinach in it, I only taste the fruit, but I get the nutrients of the spinach without tasting it! Likewise, applications like Kode Karts offer free and fun games to entice kids into learning lessons in computer science. If that's not a parenting win, I don't know what is.

If you are a parent or guardian who prefers not to use technology often with your children, first, good for you, and second, there are still tons of options for technology-free play that promote computer science skills. Toys like LEGOs promote building with small pieces to build one large object, or difficult puzzles that make your student strategize and practice resilience.

The toy industry is loaded with products that strike the balance between fun and learning–you just have to look for them. In fact, for my nephew's tenth birthday I bought him a STEM subscription box, and every few months, he gets a box in the mail with a different activity that promotes STEM learning. My nephew thinks it's the coolest present ever because he gets to tinker and create with his own hands and build a fun toy house. I think it's the coolest present ever because I get to watch my nephew establish an appreciation and love of STEM. My sisters think I'm a little nosey pushing my own passions onto their kids, but the kids are liking it, so I'm going to keep being nosey until they stop me!

When it comes to elementary students, the primary focus is to establish intellectual curiosity. If a student is able to recognize vaguely what computer science is, then they are at a tremendous advantage.

CHAPTER 8

INTO THE CLASSROOM

"Much education today is monumentally ineffective. All too often we are giving young people cut flowers when we should be teaching them to grow their own plants."

—JOHN W. GARDNER

Secondary education is where the magic really begins! As I said, computer science is not as challenging as society makes it out to be. With enough computer science knowledge and competence, a student could graduate high school and get a software developer job without a college degree.

However, most high schools do not offer enough computer science classes for a student to be a sufficiently strong enough computer programmer to land a job out of high school. But that's not the point. My point is that computer science is easy enough for *any* high school student to learn.

It would be great if every high school student were required to take at least one computer science class in high school, but I find that to be unrealistic. So, I will simply suggest that computer science courses are attainable at every high school. That said, we must address the roadblocks.

ROADBLOCKS

Of all the roadblocks, funding probably sits at the top of the list. For starters, the education sector is always in need of more funding for all the moving parts. We need to pay the teachers more, update facilities, get up-to-date textbooks, have supplies, keep the heat and lights on, and so much more. So, asking for money to get an entire room of new or updated computers and an experienced, qualified teacher doesn't always rank high on the list of priorities. Computers also depreciate fairly quickly in contrast to facility or textbook upgrades, so it's a short-term investment with a big price tag.

Another roadblock to consider is teacher availability. There are currently conversations regarding a potential teacher shortage in the United States, and computer science teachers are no exception. In fact, according to Economic Policy Institute reports, the teacher shortage is substantially worsening, especially in high-poverty areas.[19] This is especially alarming when considering the knowledge and skill required to gain a computer science teacher's license.

As mentioned, Advanced Placement (AP) computer science courses require teachers to be licensed. So, when considering

---

19 Emma García and Elaine Weiss, "The Teacher Shortage Is Real, Large and Growing, and Worse than We Thought: The First Report in 'The Perfect Storm in the Teacher Labor Market' Series."

the declining teacher population and the difficulty associated with obtaining a computer science teaching license, this is no easy feat. Which brings me to my next point: Establishing teacher motivation.

Passing a licensing exam requires teachers to possess in-depth knowledge of certain computer programming languages, software development methodologies, and more. And the icing on the cake is that computer science is constantly changing! Coding languages that were popular ten years ago are now ancient history. Well, not exactly ancient history, but definitely no longer the most relevant or frequently used language. When a high school teacher specializes in physics or algebra, not much is changing in their entire forty-year career! But if a teacher dives into a computer science specialty, they have to be prepared to master and teach an entirely new language five to ten years down the line.

Lastly, student interest is crucial for any computer science program to flourish. Convincing a student to enroll in a computer science class, especially when they have no prior experience with the subject, is a difficult task. As mentioned earlier, prevailing attitudes and stereotypes suggest that computer science is only for antisocial geniuses who code for fun in their basements. But many different kinds of people have an interest in technology and are doing great in the field. It is time to end the stigma around computer science. Anyone can do it, and like anything else, it takes time, effort, and drive, but it is far from impossible.

WHEN COMPUTER SCIENCE REACHES THE CLASSROOM

There are a few options in getting a teacher and school involved in starting a computer science education program, depending on your school's situation.

If a school has a qualified and well-supported teacher eager and ready to teach computer science, countless courses of all levels could be implemented. To start, there's Introduction to Computer Science or Web Design, also advanced courses like AP CS A or AP CS Principals. Depending on your student body, there are numerous classes to choose from, which will best ensure the teachers' and students' success. However, if classes are being added to the curriculum that means that students have to be interested and motivated to sign up and stay in those classes.

One way schools have made computer science a more enticing topic than a math or science curriculum requirement is with a computer science course. That way, students will not feel overwhelmed with an analytically heavy course load and the computer science class will have more appeal for students.

Let's say a school has an interested and supported teacher who wants to teach computer science and has the time for the course, but they are not qualified to teach the subject matter. In this case, I strongly suggest looking at the TEALS program introduced in chapter two. TEALS will prepare and support teachers as they learn to take on a computer science curriculum alongside a technology professional.

As a reminder, the goal of this program is to train a teacher to be able to confidently and effectively teach a computer science course after two years of involvement. That said, this is a great opportunity for schools who want to integrate computer science courses into the curriculum and have a teacher with the capacity to take it on.

Last, if a teacher is neither qualified nor in a school that would support the addition of a computer science course, there are ways to integrate computer science skills into any classroom. Through Code.org, there are projects called "Hour of Code," which are engaging games and activities that take approximately one hour and teach computer science skills. There are countless activities and games of all levels, so the class can differentiate depending on a student's knowledge and speed of activity.

Some downfalls of this option are that it requires a computer lab where every student has access to a desktop or laptop, and the teacher must be willing to sacrifice one hour of teaching or grading per week. Many schools in the Milwaukee area participate in "Hour of Code," but it does take planning by both the school and the teacher participating. These are just some of the many examples of bringing computer science into the high school classroom.

INSIGHTS FROM A COMPUTER SCIENCE TEACHER
I had the pleasure of speaking with one of Wisconsin's leading high school computer science teachers, Ryan Osterburg, about his experience. Ryan has worked as a math and computer science teacher at Brookfield Central High School for over twenty years and helped establish countless opportunities for his students through innovative coursework and engaging activities.

Ryan has changed and improved upon his computer science program many times, adding new opportunities for his students and making the classes more appealing for students with all types of interest. One program he started, called LAUNCH has brought students into the business world to solve real-world problems. LAUNCH is a project-based learning opportunity where students receive course credits for working on a specific project for a local business.

The students must complete AP CS A (AP Computer Science A) in order to participate in the program, and classes are usually comprised of third- and fourth-year high school students because of prerequisites and the necessity to drive to and from businesses. The program is in its third year and has now expanded to include students from the neighboring school district.

Ryan recruits any local businesses who want to participate, requiring that they have an actual business problem that could be solved by a group of high school computer science students. The business must offer several employees to help explain the business problem and assist the students in answering any questions they may have throughout the year. Additionally, the participating businesses must understand that the problem at hand will take several months to accomplish.

Granted, this is a lot to ask of a business. However, by participating, the business lends a hand in helping the local community, receives a fresh perspective and solution from their business partner, and gets to look at early talent in the area.

Once students are assigned to a group and a business solution, they are required to act as a business team would when investigating a solution and coming up with a solution. Ryan teaches students how to adequately communicate with their business stakeholders and one another, emphasizing accountability. He "wants to be the last resort when they have a question. Before students ask me, they should ask their peers and do their research and then, if they still can't find the answer, they can come find (him)." This approach makes the students accountable to one another for producing a successful business solution.

Opportunities like this allow students to practice what life would be like working in a technology job. By giving the students real-world business problems that can be solved using computer science, students can experience the relevance of the work they've done in school. Additionally, opportunities like the LAUNCH program get students excited about a potential career in computer science. With such a high demand for computer science jobs, getting students excited about it as a possible career path can help fill that demand while ensuring a fun and stable future for that student.

Computer science in high schools is critical when it comes to bringing young people into the profession. If high schools can provide access to the numerous computer science education, students will be better prepared for a successful future.

CHAPTER 9

LEARNING COMPUTER SCIENCE AS AN ADULT

"Live as if you were to die tomorrow. Learn as if you were to live forever."

—MAHATMA GANDHI

When was the last time you sat down to learn something completely new?

For me, it hasn't been since college. I am a few years out of college now and am planning on going back to graduate school in a few months. In preparation for my program, I am required to take several courses to ensure I am prepared for the rigorous coursework ahead. One of the classes I'm taking is a college statistics overview. The last statistics class I took was about five years ago, and it's safe to say I retained *none* of that information because, in my defense, I don't really use statistics in my everyday life. While taking the course, I find myself multi-tasking and retaining about half of what the instructional videos say. I think it's fair to say I'm going to have to relearn how to be a student.

A growing population of people working outside of the tech sector is curious about learning computer science. Fortunately enough, there are a growing number of opportunities catered to adults looking to learn these skills. Throughout the book so far, I have discussed fairly traditional ways to integrate computer science skills and coursework into the classroom.

But what about people who want to learn computer science who are no longer in high school? How do they go about learning computer science and relearning how to be a student?

THE JOURNEY
Deciding to switch careers as an adult is courageous. Many people wanting to learn computer science have either graduated college with a non-tech-related degree or did not attend or complete college in the first place. The entire technology field is homogeneous, and educational equity has a lot to do with that. However, anyone at any time, age, and with any educational background can begin learning computer science if they have the drive and resourcefulness. Carlos Vasquez, who was introduced earlier, started his software development journey after several years in the workforce.

Carlos joined a year-long program for adults from diverse backgrounds to learn computer science and prepare for software development careers. Granted, this program required him to quit his job, work successfully for the program, and acquire a completely new skill, which is a lot of effort. Upon graduating, Carlos created his own application and built a career out of Habla Code.

Carlos exemplifies many other adults who return to school to study computer science and build a new career. He took a risk and invested in himself, and his reward has been a passionate career that enables others to learn computer science skills as well. There are many opportunities to learn computer science–from in-person classes to online self-taught courses–that are worth looking into and taking advantage of.

Another resource that I use every so often to refresh my memory or learn a new language is Codecademy (I pronounce it "code-academy"). I used Codecademy in college to reinforce the languages I was learning in class. My professor probably wouldn't have approved because I didn't adhere to his best practices, but I enjoyed it regardless. Some courses are free, and others charge a fee, depending on the depth of the material.

Codecademy functions like a virtual multimedia classroom with video lessons, quizzes, games, and other activities. The program charges a monthly subscription rate and requires a computer and internet access. People with or without regular computer or Wi-Fi access can also access their local public library. Libraries often have after-school activities for children of all ages and even adult tutors, so it is definitely worth checking out. Codecademy offers a more structured approach to learning computer science.

After graduating high school, I went to college with the hope of becoming an athletic trainer. There was no reason for me to pursue athletic training beyond fitness and thinking it would be a fun career choice, but there was no passion behind my decision. After a year of taking classes, I realized I had chosen the wrong course of study, so I entered business school with an "undecided" major. My business school counselor picked out all my classes for the semester, and Introduction to Information Technology happened to be one of them.

Shortly after enrolling, I realized that I really enjoyed technology. Innovation and opportunities perpetuated growth everywhere I turned, and it was exciting to finally have found a career path I could see myself pursuing. I'm extremely grateful to have been placed in a technology course at the right time. Oftentimes, collegiate introductory information technology or computer science courses can be taken as an elective, which are required for many majors.

At the risk of sounding like a broken record, computer technology courses are useful in nearly every career, so simply taking a technology-related course as a college elective is a great field of study for college students.

WHAT ARE YOUR OPTIONS?
Studying technology as an elective is an awesome option for those college students. I should mention though that college courses are expensive, so taking a course to simply explore a subject may not be feasible for many people. So if you can, take a college introductory course in technology or computer science and you will learn a lot. But, if that's not in the cards for you, there are other options.

Another option would be to enroll in a fast-track coding course. There are many in-person class opportunities for learning how to program and preparing to work in the field after just a few weeks or months. This option would probably be the most expensive, but it allows students to attend in-person lessons, have the guidance of a real teacher with technology experience, and have the fastest turnaround time for getting a job. These programs also often supply computers with all the necessary software and hardware already installed, so all you need to do is show up and pay attention.

It is important to note that these programs are designed for those looking to master computer programming languages with the intention of going into the field upon course completion. If you are looking to learn computer science for fun, this is probably an intense and expensive way to go about it.

For those looking to learn computer science for the fun of it or looking to increase skills and awareness, there are plenty of free options out there. All the aforementioned resources for students, such as Code.org, are also great for adults. The internet has thousands of free resources to explore, even if you're finished with your formal education.

There are plenty of options for adults to learn computer science but changing career paths can be difficult. Relearning how to be a student rather than a professional is also difficult. Unlike most traditional students who are only responsible for themselves and their studies, adults balance a multitude of responsibilities, such as work, caring for their families, and paying their bills all while taking a chance on this new skill. Also, after someone learns a programming language, they will need to start at an entry level position. People cannot come into a position with no relevant work experience and expect to land a leadership role. Those promotions take time and climbing the ladder can be a difficult transition.

REALISTIC EXPECTATIONS

Like anything in life, studying computer science offers no guarantees. People in technology careers sometimes don't like their job, programming can be boring for others, and even in an era of booming technology, market layoffs still happen. Switching career paths is a risk and though it comes with many rewards, it's still a risk. When you have a family to support and a steady job that pays enough, it can be a really tough to leave and invest in computer science. But from what I've seen, it's worth it.

CHAPTER 10

TIME TO ACT

"Be the change that you wish to see in the world."

—MAHATMA GANDHI

This book has discussed the benefits of computer science skills and education at length. You already know the relevance and advantages computer science education brings and you already know that by implementing more technology lessons into the classroom, more students will have the ability to invest in the field's potential.

Clearly, though, it is not easy to get new courses into the classroom. Computer science advocacy must come from multiple sources in order to convince influential people that it is worth the time, effort, and money. Everyone is different, and advocacy will look different depending on who you are. The most important thing is to act in any way you can. Every conversation helps get us closer to equitable computer science opportunities for all.

THE STUDENT

If you are a high school student, and you want to see computer science at your school or take computer science classes at your school, there are a handful of ways to get involved:

1. Even when you think you don't have much of a voice, it is crucial that you SAY SOMETHING anyway! Contrary to common belief, adults do not know everything. Having a respectful and well-researched conversation with the right adults can lead to monumental change. Talk to your teachers and administration to demonstrate your interest in computer science and follow up if needed. In many cases, schools mistakenly think they are providing the best technology program when, in fact, all they are providing is great equipment. If a computer science course is only available once a year and it conflicts with schedules, share that information, too.
2. If you are itching to get your hands dirty in computer science now, join an extracurricular coding program! There are cool opportunities outside of the classroom for high school students to learn, practice, and master computer science. Clubs like Girls Who Code, business sponsored Hack-a-thons, or other local programs are hungry for interested students! Do a quick search on availability and opportunities in your area and get involved. If you can't find a program in your city, reach out to clubs like Girl Scouts, Boy Scouts, Girls Who Code, or Boys and Girls Club, and they can either point you in the right direction or help implement a new program for your city.
3. I highly recommend that every student find a mentor. Mentorship creates awesome connections between professionals and students and can provide the advice, resources,

and tools that will help you succeed. If you have even the slightest interest in computer science, whether you want to become a software engineer or just want to learn more about it, connecting with an adult in the profession can be enlightening.

Mentors are always a good idea, but in computer science particularly, a mentor can teach you about the countless technology opportunities and current innovations or maybe even lead you to a future job! You never know where one cup of coffee may lead.

THE PARENT

Before I even start recommending ways for parents to act and get involved, I feel it's important to clarify that I am not a parent. As a young professional, I can only draw from my close relationship with my parents and my sisters who have children. I will try and be as practical and understanding as possible, with full knowledge that this advice might not work for all kids. (Feel free to try these strategies and get back to me, or just laugh quietly to yourself about my naiveté. Either works.) Here are some action parents can take to make a change:

1. Join your school's PTA to have a voice in your student's school.

   You don't need to attend every meeting from now until eternity, bringing computer science opportunities to the attention of other parents can raise awareness and grow support from those with the same priorities as you. What is important to the parents becomes important to the schools, so make your voice heard! Detail why including computer science educational opportunities to students is so beneficial and add how you think the school can accomplish this. I'm guessing that you will not be the only parent who will see its importance and join you in the fight.

2. I highly recommend supporting computer science activities outside of school.

   Bring your student to work with you and introduce them to your IT team. Have them explain what they do and how they got into their position.

3. Offer to drive your student to a hack-a-thon across town so they can experience coding with other students their age. These may be little actions but showing excitement for computer science will make your student more excited as well. It will take courage on your student's part and time on your part, but these activities can open doors to career paths, scholarships, friendships, and so much more.

4. Initiate conversation. Ask your student what they find interesting and why.

   The answers to those questions will probably, in one way or another, tie back to computer science whether that be fashion, healthcare, or business. See if your student has interest in taking a computer science class or pursuing a future job in that field someday. Sparking the conversation is crucial to make sure you and your student are on the same page.

THE TEACHER

I am glorifying and calling on teachers throughout this entire book. And if you haven't noticed, I suggest you reread the entire book because you definitely missed the point. Anyway, teachers, you play an incredible role in the lives of students, and I'm so grateful that you do what you do. Here are some ideas to help you integrate computer science either as a course or even tomorrow in your classroom. Here are some steps you can take to make a change:

1. Start by talking to your administration.
   Having a productive discussion with your school explaining what computer science is and what your school can do to implement it could be the game changer. It will also help you in understanding your specific school and the struggles it faces. Understanding the "why" behind tough issues like bringing in a pricey and time-consuming course that'll have a great impact on students will help you be a better advocate. Additionally, having these conversations will force you and your administration to ask the tough questions. If you feel uncomfortable having this conversation alone with administration, bring a buddy. Having an ally who also works in your school in the room always calms fears and makes you feel like you have an advantage. This conversation with coworkers will plant the seed in their heads and hopefully start a movement for more computer science classes.
2. Enroll and participate in a computer science teaching workshop.
   This task is easier for some teachers than others depending on where they are located and their state's accessibility for computer science teacher trainings. However, it is worth an internet search to see if there are any opportunities near your area. Many times, your school district will pay for the workshop, and if they will not pay for it, there are many sponsors that give scholarships for these types of workshops like Code.org, Google, and Microsoft to name a few. Speak with the workshop organizers to get you in touch with one of their sponsors. This option

depends largely on time and money for teachers so it may not be feasible for everyone.
3. If you are especially eager and want to do something now, integrate technology today.

While researching for this book, I spoke with many teachers (mostly in STEM fields) about their relationship with bringing computer science lessons into the classroom. Overwhelmingly, I heard of something many different schools are implementing called Hour of Code or Technology Hour. Hour of Code is a voluntary hour in which teachers dedicate every Friday (or whatever day of the week) for their students to explore computer science. Many teachers use Code.org as their Hour of Code resource, but many other resources are available. This method does require a teacher to forfeit an entire class of regular lessons, but when a school does not offer computer science opportunities, this one hour a week can be eye opening for many students. Hour of Code differentiates lessons, so those first starting out and master coders can finish a project in an hour.

1. If you don't have an entire hour a week to dedicate to computer science, build it into your course.
Computer science can be integrated into almost any course as it appears in every field and has so many capabilities. By relating a class topic to computer science and raising awareness of where computer science can fit into different aspects of different subject, it gives your students the chance to explore possibilities within the topic.
2. Be an advocate and resource!
Talk about integrating computer science into your classes with other teachers and encourage them to explore the

same opportunities. One of the more difficult aspects of teaching computer science or integrating computer science into the classroom is that there are rarely other teachers in your school doing the same. By getting the ball rolling and creating a community within your school, more teachers will feel more ready and supported to try giving computer science integration a shot. If you or other teachers are also facing a lack of resources, check out the CSTA (Computer Science Teachers Association).

The CSTA strives to serve as a resource to support computer science teachers, and those teachers wanting to integrate more computer science into their lesson plans. Exploring and sharing resources can help widen the reach of students who get the chance to experience a computer science education, whether that is through a computer science course or through the integration of computer science in their other classes.

THE TECHNOLOGY PROFESSIONAL

I'm going to have some fun talking to technology professionals because I am a part of this group. These recommendations come from my experience both as a technology student and professional. Please take some time to consider these options for computer science advocacy because YOU ended up in this field somehow and perhaps someone else is looking for the inspiration to do the same. Here are some actions you can take to make a change:

1. I have already talked about it so much, but I can't recommend it enough: join TEALS!
   There is a reason I have brought it up in so many chapters in this book. It is an amazing organization. You choose

a school to volunteer at, I usually pick a school between my home and my work and show up for first hour twice a week. In my experience, high schools operate much earlier than workplaces, so by the time first hour is done at 8:30am, I jump in my car make it to work by 8:45am. Two hours a week is all you need to make a world of difference in a student's life. It is a yearly commitment, which I realize is a long time, but volunteering reaffirms my love of technology and motivates my work. Please investigate it. TEALS is an incredible program doing amazing work for the community.

2. If TEALS sounds like too much for you, try volunteering. I realize joining TEALS is volunteering, but I thought the two categories should be separated because volunteering at one-off events and a year-long commitment are different.

   Volunteer at a hack-a-thon, for a Girl Scout or Boy Scout troop earning their STEM badge, or any of the other countless organizations looking for experienced CS professionals. I like to volunteer with my public libraries doing the Hour of Code program, but be sure to pick something you genuinely like. There are also FIRST Robotics teams always looking for coaches and volunteers and would greatly benefit from someone with experience in the technology field. Search for opportunities, say yes, and commit to helping.

3. If you are going to take any single piece of advice, please let it be this one: be a mentor.

   Serve as a mentor for a student interested in computer science. Take them out for coffee or lunch and talk about why you became interested in the field, how you got to where you are today, and what keeps you engaged.

Invite your student to see your workplace and meet your co-workers. Mentoring students opens their eyes to exciting career options and the confidence that they, too, can succeed. It also helps for students to know that they can go on this journey of becoming a technology professional and they will not be alone in it.

I found my mentor during my first job when she was my manager. After she left the company, we kept in touch, and I eventually followed her to her new job. I am so grateful to have found someone I can look up to and talk to because it is a game changer having someone to give you the truth while always looking out for your best interests.

AS A CITIZEN

If you do not fall into any of the previous categories and you want to get involved, there are still ways to advocate for computer science opportunities within your community:

1. Volunteering is a surefire way to show your support and promote technology events.
   You do not need to be familiar with computer programming in order to help increase opportunities into your community. Oftentimes, hack-a-thons and public libraries hosting computer science events need volunteers to help set up, sign students in, serve lunch, and so on. It may not be glamorous, but it needs to be done. By volunteering your time, you are showing the community that you value computer science opportunities for all students.
2. Something that should not be forgotten or played down is the power of donating.
   There are countless organizations—Code.org, Girls Who Code, TEALSk12, and so on that are non-profit

organizations working to bring computer science opportunities to all students. Your donation helps provide relevant content, hire advocates in different regions, and so much more. By financially supporting these organizations, you can do your part without knowing anything about computer science.

ANYONE CAN HELP

Everyone plays a role in advocating for equitable computer science opportunities in their communities. Whether it be a small conversation, a donation, integrating computer science into your day-to-day life as a parent or teacher, or volunteering, every action gets us one step closer to achieving our goal. Just by reading this book and raising your own awareness of the issue of low computer science opportunity, you are contributing to this goal. Go you!

CONCLUSION
WHAT NOW?

Throughout writing this book, I had countless conversations with different professionals, in tech and otherwise, and I received similar feedback from almost everyone: I'm so passionate about computer science education that I have tunnel vision about achieving my goals. Some self-reflection and a glass of wine later, I realize that this tunnel vision is blocking me from seeing a lot.

For the longest time, I wanted to end my book with a list of reasons why bringing computer science education opportunities to every classroom is a pipe dream. I would discuss how the lack of diversity in the technology field will only grow if something isn't done to encourage people of color and women to explore the field, and I would emphasize the need for more computer science teachers and programs.

But I ultimately decided to not let readers walk away from my book thinking about all the obstacles to greater access. Instead, I want to thank everyone who is working tirelessly to promote greater access to computer science education and the tech industry. Let us celebrate the everyday wins and accomplishments!

Thank you to those who are taking the big and small steps necessary to bring us closer to computer science educational equity. My dream is ultimately to see a flourishing and diverse technology workforce that utilizes tech advances to serve the common good. We are closer to that goal today than we were yesterday, and tomorrow we'll be even closer.

BIBLIOGRAPHY

Preface

"Computer And Information Technology Occupations : Occupational Outlook Handbook: : U.S. Bureau Of Labor Statistics." 2020. *Bls.gov*. https://www.bls.gov/ooh/computer-and-information-technology/home.htm.

"The Integrated Postsecondary Education Data System." 2020. *Nces.ed.gov*. https://nces.ed.gov/ipeds.

"What's Wrong With This Picture?" 2020. *Code.org*. https://code.org/promote.

Introduction

N/A

Chapter 1

"AP Data – Research – College Board." 2020. *Research*. Accessed September 2019. https://research.collegeboard.org/programs/ap/data.

"Illustrating Equality VS Equity." Illustrating Equality VS Equity : Interaction Institute for Social Change. Accessed September 2019. https://interactioninstitute.org/illustrating-equality-vs-equity/.

"Information Technology." *Data USA*. Accessed August 2019. https://datausa.io/profile/cip/information-technology#demographics

Johnson, Brandi. Achievement Gap in Education, June 18, 2014. https://blogs.longwood.edu/bradleybl/2014/06/18/achievement-gap-defined/.

Ott, Lindsey. "Solving the Achievement Gap Through Equity, Not Equality." *TED*. Accessed September 2019. https://www.ted.com/talks/lindsey_ott_solving_the_achievement_gap_through_equity_not_equality.

Safier, Rebecca. "Complete Guide: Colleges Not Requiring SAT Scores." Complete Guide: Colleges Not Requiring SAT Scores. Accessed September 2019. https://blog.prepscholar.com/the-complete-guide-to-sat-optional-colleges.

Chapter 2

"Software Engineer." 2020. *Glassdoor.com*. Accessed August 2019. https://www.glassdoor.com/Salaries/software-engineer-salary-SRCH_KO0,17.htm.

"Trades, Skilled, and Skilled Trades." 2020. "How Much Does Skilled Trades Pay? | Indeed.Com." *Indeed.com*. Accessed August 2019. https://www.indeed.com/cmp/Skilled-Trades/salaries.

"Student Loan Debt Statistics In 2019: A $1.5 Trillion Crisis." 2020. *Forbes.com*. Accessed August 2019. https://www.forbes.com/sites/zackfriedman/2019/02/25/student-loan-debt-statistics-2019/#4522b170133f.

Chapter 3
N/A

Chapter 4
N/A

Chapter 5
"Blurbs and Useful Stats." 2020. *Csed Week*. https://csedweek.org/resource_kit/blurbs.

Chapter 6
"About TEALS - What Is TEALS?" *Microsoft*. Accessed September 2019. https://www.microsoft.com/en-us/teals/about.

Adkins, Amy. "Millennials: The Job-Hopping Generation." Gallup.com. Gallup, December 16, 2019. https://www.gallup.com/workplace/231587/millennials-job-hopping-generation.aspx.

Carver-Thomas, D. & L. Darling-Hammond. (2017). *Teacher turnover: Why it matters and what we can do about it*. Palo Alto, CA: Learning Policy Institute. Accessed September 2019. https://learningpolicyinstitute.org/sites/default/files/product-files/Teacher_Turnover_REPORT.pdf.

Gallup, Inc. 2020. "Millennials: The Job-Hopping Generation." *Gallup.com*. https://www.gallup.com/workplace/231587/millennials-job-hopping-generation.aspx.

"Information Technology." *Data USA*. Accessed August 2019. https://datausa.io/profile/cip/information-technology#demographics.

Chapter 7
N/A

Chapter 8
García, Emma, and Elaine Weiss. "The Teacher Shortage Is Real, Large and Growing, and Worse than We Thought: The First Report in 'The Perfect Storm in the Teacher Labor Market' Series." *Economic Policy Institute*. Accessed March 27, 2020. https://www.epi.org/publication/the-teacher-shortage-is-real-large-and-growing-and-worse-than-we-thought-the-first-report-in-the-perfect-storm-in-the-teacher-labor-market-series/. *Economic Policy Institute*. Accessed August 2019. https://www.epi.org/publication/the-teacher-shortage-is-real-large-and-growing-and-worse-than-we-thought-the-first-report-in-the-perfect-storm-in-the-teacher-labor-market-series/.

Chapter 9
N/A

Chapter 10
N/A

Conclusion
N/A

www.ingramcontent.com/pod-product-compliance
Lightning Source LLC
LaVergne TN
LVHW011846060526
838200LV00054B/4199